N Queens Perimeter Method

A New Approach to the n Queens Puzzle

Norm Hult

PREFACE

"The last thing one discovers in composing a work is what to put first." — Blaise Pascal

In this book I will show you how to create a list of 108 seed starting positions which will resolve to all 92 solutions of the 8 queens puzzle.

I will describe my thought processes which lead to this simple method.

I will explain why the 108 seeds are logically guaranteed to contain all the total solutions.

I will show how a seed is used to isolate the solutions and the rejects.

I have implemented these ideas into a C++ program and confirmed the results on grids from 4x4 up to 15x15.

This book assumes you are familiar with the n Queens puzzle.

Rows	Fundamental Solutions	Total Solutions
4	1	2
5	2	10
6	1	4
7	6	40
8	12	92
9	46	352
10	92	724
11	341	2680
12	1787	14200
13	9233	73712
14	45752	365596
15	285053	2279184
16	1846955	14772512

I would like to thank friends and family who have listened to me talk about this idea for what seems like forever. An extra special thank-you to my wonderful wife Jackie. Your love and patience and incredible editing skills helped me finish this project.

Eight Queens

The Eight Queens Problem

Imagine a King with an imaginary square island, which happens to be divided into 64 equally sized estates. Like a giant chess board.

Because this king could not decide among the eight most beautiful ladies of his court, he unwisely decides to marry all eight. Now we have eights Queens.

Each queen demanded her own estate. There are 64 estates. The solution should be easy. Each queen also demanded a clear view to the coast south, west, north, and east. And she demanded a clear view to the coast diagonally in each direction. Not so easy.

Computer programmers will recognize the king's dilemma as an example of the problem named "n queens", often used to discuss the broader topic of "P versus NP." The n queens problem is classified as NP, meaning Non-Polynomial time. If a solution is **hard to find,** but it is **easy to check**, it's NP!

Simple math indicates there are 4,426,165,368 different ways you can place 8 distinct queens on a chess board if there were no demands about clear views.

But when the Queens demands are met, in the end, there are only 92 total solutions.

These 92 solutions contain similarities that break down into 12 fundamental solutions.

This has been known since 1850!

This book is not really about the 92 solutions.

This book is about analyzing the problem, applying logic, and developing an algorithm to solve it.

We will test our logic against grids in the range of 4x4 to 16x16.

The n Queens Puzzle

Several computer algorithms already exist to solve n Queens.

There is a structured approach, a brute force algorithm, a permutation method, backtracking depth search, and pruning.

Permutation Method

Computer programmers applied the "One Queen Per Row, One Queen Per Column" rules and narrowed the 4.4 billion number down to a more manageable 40,320 potential solutions, which are then checked diagonally.

Backtracking Depth Search and Pruning

Backtracking Depth Search examines 15,720 potential solutions. A further improvement called pruning examines 5,508 solutions. We have gone from

4,426,165,368 potential solutions down to 40,320 potential solutions, then down to 15,720 potential solutions and finally down to 5,508 potential solutions.

Can we do better? I think yes! How about 108 potential starting positions?

These 108 potential solutions are not chosen at random. They are chosen from a method which logically guarantees you will find all fundamental solutions. From these you calculate the total solutions.

Any single solution can be considered a fundamental solution. It can then be rotated several times, mirrored, and then rotated several more times to make up the total solutions for that one fundamental. In most cases, the single fundamental becomes 8 total solutions. However, if the fundamental solution is symmetrical, the mirrored image will be the same as the original image. In this case it only becomes 4 total solutions,

Perimeter

Perimeter – a new logical method

May I repeat that this book is not actually about the solutions. The 92 solutions for an 8x8 grid are already known. This book describes my quest to find a new logical method, an algorithm, to find these solutions, and to share my process of doing this with you.

I arrived at this new method, which I think of as a **Perimeter** method, on my own. I have Googled for similar approaches, and I have found nothing like it. If it exists, I am not aware of it.

As described above, the number of potential solutions for an 8x8 grid has gone from 4.4 billion potentials, down to 40K potentials, down to 15K, and finally down to 5K.

Can we do better?

We will develop a way of identifying 108 potential starting positions.

Logically all 12 fundamental solutions are in these 108 starting positions.

By evaluating each of these starting positions will find all 12 of the fundamental solutions.

We will reject the remaining starting points.

Starting with these fundamental solutions, by using rotation and mirroring we will derive the full 92 total solutions.

My Goals

My goal for this book is to demonstrate how to create an algorithm to solve for a specific problem, n Queens.

I am using the example of n Queens with a set of goals in mind.

1. I want the reader to learn to look at the problem with fresh eyes, develop a solution from the ground up.

2. I want to walk the reader through all the steps from developing an idea to creating a solution and testing the results.

3. I want the resulting program to work for grids sized from 4 x 4 to 16 x 16 *. The only change to the program will be the size of the grid.

5. I will use an 8 x 8 for the discussion and development. The solutions are well known are and easily found (see Appendix 1a). I can test the code against the known results.

6. I want to demonstrate analyzing the puzzle, developing an algorithm, and writing code to implement the algorithm.

There are many ways to look at a puzzle and write an algorithm to solve it.

This is just one.

* I successfully tested 4x4 to 15x15 grids. The 16x16 file was too large to sort on my laptop, so my results for this 16x16 grid size are unknown at this time.

Conventions

Row and Column:

Rows are numbered, bottom to top.

Row count starts at 1.

Columns are numbered, left to right.

Column count starts at 1.

Example:

The dark square is at row 4, column 6.

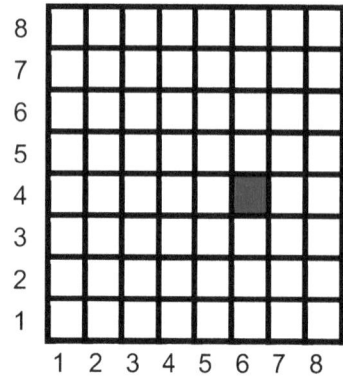

Position:

Squares in the grid can be referred to by position. The position calculation is Row multiplied by a scaling factor of 100, plus the column number. Here the dark square is at position 406.

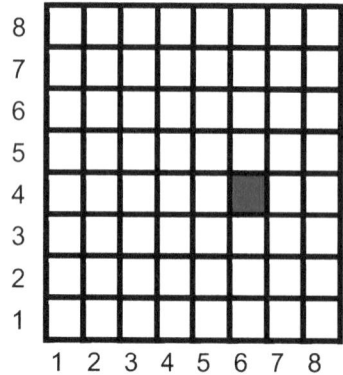

The total number of squares on each row and column of the grid is referred to as nsquares,

On our 64 square grid, this is 8 x 8, thus nsquares = 8.

Conventions continued

Positions (alternate):

For some purposes, mainly in examples, I will refer to positions in this alternate way:

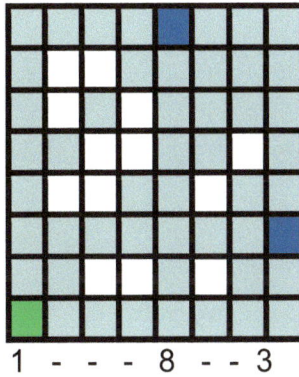

The numbers below the grid show, for each column, which row is occupied by a queen. The current state of this board is 1 - - - 8 - - 3.

This translates as:

In column 1, a queen is on row 1.
Columns 2, 3, and 4 have no queen yet.
In column 5, there is a queen on row 8.
Columns 6 and 7 have no queen yet.
Column 8 has a queen on row 3.

I use this for demonstrations and explanations only, I will not be using this convention in code.

Conventions continued…

Left Diagonal, variable name ldiag:

The left diagonals are numbered 1 to 15 on an 8x8 grid.

In code, the "15" is determined with the calc (nsquares*2)-1

It is calculated so the program can be run for various grid sizes.

Here the dark square at row 4, column 6 resolves to a Left Diagonal of 10.

Left Diagonal can be calculated as:

 Column + row.

Here 4 + 6 = 10

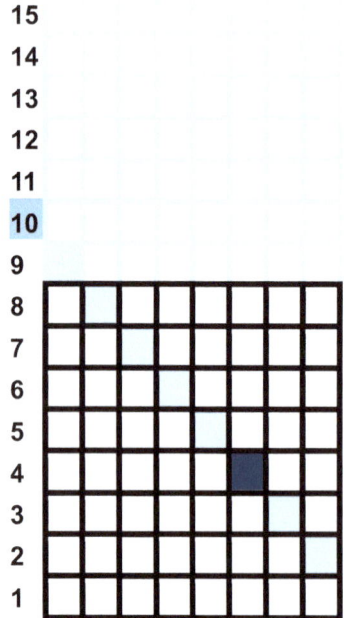

Conventions continued…

Right Diagonal, variable name rdiag:

The right diagonals are numbered 1 to 15 for an 8x8 grid.

The "15" value is determined by the calculation (nsquares*2)-1.

Here the dark square at row 4, column 6 resolves to a Right Diagonal of 7.

Right Diagonal can be calculated as:

Row + (nsquares – col) + 1

Here (8 – 6) + 1 = 7

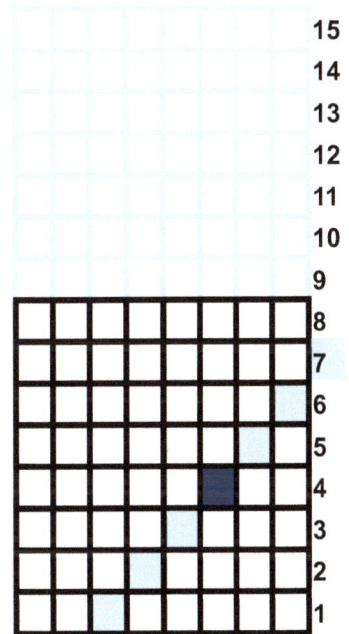

Learn The n Queen Rules

Each Queen gets her own Row.

In our program we will use a C++ array to keep track of which rows have a queen. We can then skip those rows easily inside a loop when we are searching for the placement of new queens.

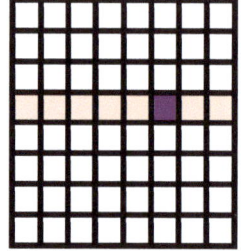

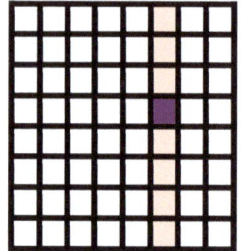

Each Queen gets her own Column.

Again, we will use an array to keep track of which columns have a queen. We can then skip those columns easily inside a loop when we are searching for the placement of new queens.

Each Queen gets her own Left Diagonal and Right Diagonal.

We will also use arrays to track protected left diagonals and right diagonals. We can easily check an open row / column position to see if that square is protected diagonally by another queen on the board.

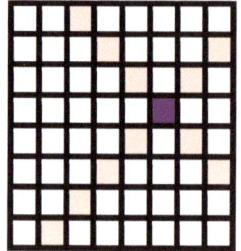

The number of Rows will always equal the number of Columns. The Grid will always be square.

Number of rows and columns can be in the range of 4-16, even and odd numbers.

An 8x8 grid will be used for demonstrations and codedevelopment.

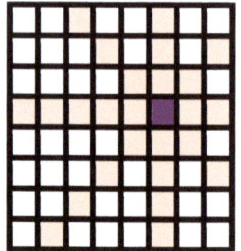

The Queen on Row 5, Column 6, controls all these squares.

No other Queen can be in a square controlled by another Queen.

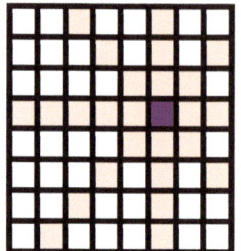

Rotation And Mirroring

Rotation and Mirroring: One solution can yield up to 8 solutions

Example: Any solution can be called a "fundamental." By using rotation and mirroring you will find another 7 solutions. Note that any one of these could have been the fundamental, and from any one of these you could find the other 7. Note: if a solution is symmetrical, you will only have a total of 4 solutions, due to the mirror image being the same as the fundamental.

Fundamental	1st Rotation	2nd Rotation	3rd Rotation

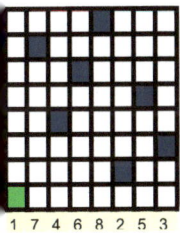 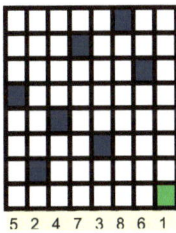 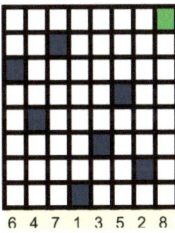 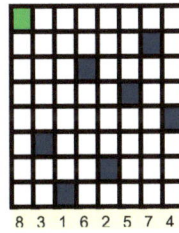

1 7 4 6 8 2 5 3   5 2 4 7 3 8 6 1   6 4 7 1 3 5 2 8   8 3 1 6 2 5 7 4

Mirror of Fundamental	1st Rotation of Mirror	2nd Rotation of Mirror	3rd Rotaton of Mirror

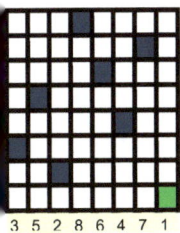 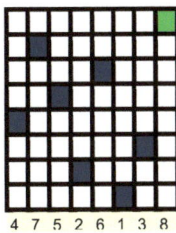 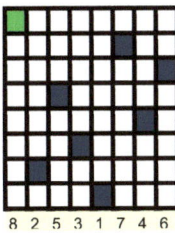 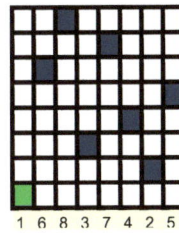

3 5 2 8 6 4 7 1   4 7 5 2 6 1 3 8   8 2 5 3 1 7 4 6   1 6 8 3 7 4 2 5

Make Observations

Your first step is to really look at the grid and the set of rules you have been given. Get out a chess board and the eight pawns (as queen substitutes since you only get two queens) and move them around a while. Try to place the Queens according to the rules. Get a feel for what you are up against. Make notes as ideas present themselves. You will not know which observations will lead to a solution.

Some of my initial observations:

A square with an even number of rows and columns can be divided into four divisions. An 8x8 grid is four 4x4 sections. In looking at the fundamentals, the eight queens are often distributed evenly in these divisions, two Queens each. But not always. Interesting, but is it useful? In the end, I did not use this observation.

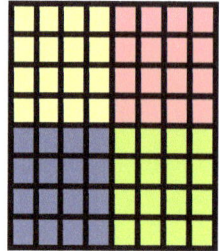

A square with an odd number of rows and columns can be divided into four divisions with a bottom to top and left to right corridor. A 7x7 grid is four 3x3 sections. A single queen in the center square controls both corridors, and of course her left and right diagonals. Interesting, but is it useful? Do we want or need different rules for even versus odd grids? I did not end up using this observation either.

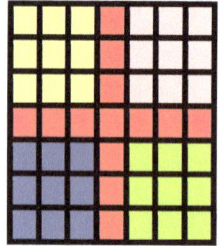

Plot the right diagonals of a valid solution, this example is Fundamental 2.
Is there a pattern to the spacing of used and unused diagonals? An even distribution between the upper and lower right diagonal halves?
Would plotting right and left diagonals for all the fundamentals help?
This is another observation I did not end up using.

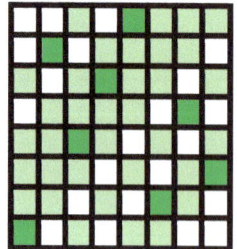

Initial Observations Continued:

A grid is a square with 4 sides: a top and bottom, and a left and right. A row must be protected by a queen, and a column must be protected by a queen.
So there must be a minimum of 3 and a maximum of 4 queens in the perimeter..I wonder how many combinations there are for an 8x8 grid?
Is it 8x8x8x8 = 4096? Fewer? **This observation is a keeper!**

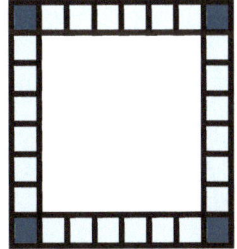

Where do I place the first queen?
On an 8x8 grid, each square has a 1 in 64 chance of being the first queen. Place a queen at Row 5 Column 6.
Remove all the **protected** squares from consideration. The remaining squares each have a 1 in 38 chance of being a queen. Is this useful? Might a statistical approach help? I rejected this idea.

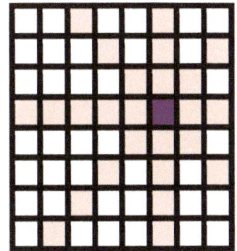

Place a queen at Row 2 Column 3, shown here in green. Now rotate the board several times.
The queen will appear to have been in several "new" locations.
However, if you move with the board, the queen does not appear to move. **This is another keeper!**

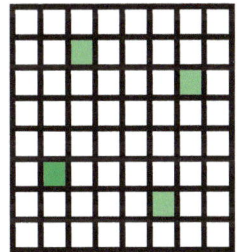

Mirror the Queens starting position to Row 3 Col 7, here in yellow. Again, rotate the board several times.
Note that the yellow square will appear to be in several new locations. A plot of the Original position and it's rotations and mirrors will be symmetrical. If a correct solution has a Queen at Row 3 Column 2,
it can be thought of as a fundamental solution, and rotated and mirrored to find another 7 solutions.
This idea is huge!

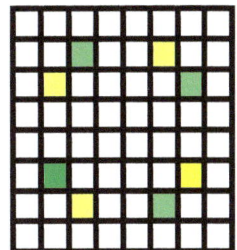

Create Your Ideas

Based on my random observations, I created these ideas

If one square can be in eight places, then one solution can also.
I am not looking for 92 total solutions, I am looking for 12 fundamental solutions. From these 12 fundamentals, I can rotate and mirror to get the 92. We know this from Rotation and Mirroring.

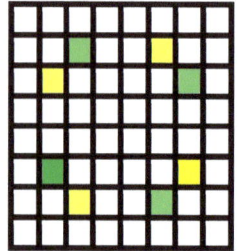

Sit four people around a chess board and ask them to to place a Queen in Row 1, Column 2. You get four "different" answers, yet each one is correct. If the board is glass and they all lay on the ground and place a Queen at Row 1, Column 2 from that perspective, you will get 4 more "different" answers. Again, all correct!

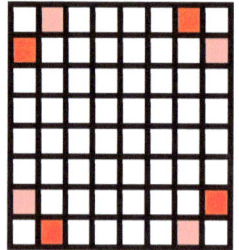

Combine the above with this idea:
The outside perimeter must be at least 3 and at most 4 queens. There is a finite number of ways to place these queens. Row 1 Columns 1 to 4 will cover the outside perimeter. Row 1, Columns 1 to 4 are our control starting points. Every combination of each of these four with the other sides will contain all possible perimeters.

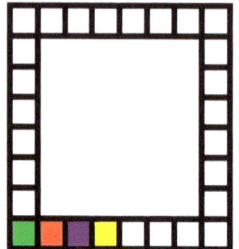

A Queen in Row 1 Col 1 protects the first Row and the First Column, as well as the diagonal from 1-1 to 8-8. Test every combination of left and top open positions, we will not need to test every mirror and rotation. We will explore later how these starting 3 or 4 queen positions lead to solutions.

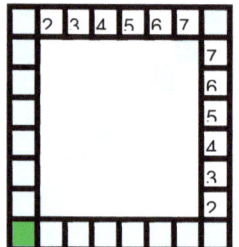

The Perimeter Method
Bottom Row, Left Column
Top Row, Right Column
(BLTR)

1	2	3	4	4	3	2	1
2							2
3							3
4							4
4							4
3							3
2							2
1	2	3	4	4	3	2	1

On an 8x8 grid, we will create a list of all the possible Bottom row, Left column, Top row, and Right column combinations where a Queen is in one of the first four squares on the bottom row. **Think of this as a "lower left orientation" process.**

Why are we only considering the first four columns of the first row?

It is due to rotation and mirroring.

Examine this grid. Note how on the bottom row, 1234 mirrors to 4321.

If you rotate the first four positions, mirror and again rotate, you will see that the bottom row 1234 covers all the outside perimeter possibilities from the lower left perspective.

If we find all the perimeter combinations that start with 1234, we have covered the entire board.

The Perimeter Method BLTR continued

Row 1 Column 1

A Queen at Row 1 Column 1 protects the bottom side and the left side.

Also, she protects the right diagonal from the lower left corner to the upper right corner.

This Queen can be combined with the remaining possibilities for the Top side and the Right side. Hold the Queens position static at Row 1 Column 1. There are six openings on the Right and six on the top. At first glance, six times six is 36 possibilities, so we put all 36 into a table.

Now look at diagonal conflicts. If you place a queen on right 2 and top 2, you will have 2 queens on the same diagonal, which is against the rules. You may only have one queen per diagonal. The Right & Top combinations of 2-2, 3-3, 4-4, 5-5, 6-6, and 7-7 are all rejects, due to this diagonal conflict. Take those 6 away and we are down to 30 possible combinations. In the next section I will show how this list of possibilities narrows down to 15 combinations.

The table for Row 1 Column 1, due to rotation and mirroring, will cover all possible results where a queen is in any one of the four corners. Later I will show how the list is used to find the solutionos.

The Perimeter Method BLTR continued

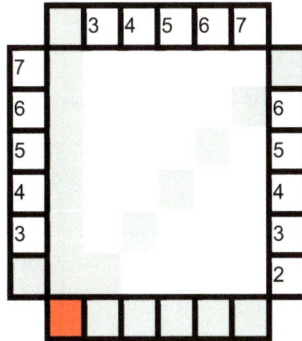

Row 1 Column 2

Place A Queen at Row 1 Column 2.

Note that the four corners are done in the previous step. There will be no corners in the Row 1 Column two possibilities table,

Create a list of all possibilities for Left Column, Top Row, and Right Side where the bottom row is held constant at Row 1 Column 2. There will be in total 125 combinations.

There will be diagonal conflicts between the left column and top row. You can only have one queen per diagonal, so Left Top combinations of 3-6, 4-5, 5-4, and 6-3 are invalid.

There are also diagonal conflicts between right and top due to the rule only one queen per diagonal, Right Top combinations of 3-3, 4-4, 5-5, and 6-6 are invalid.

There can only be one queen per row. Left Right combinations of 3-3, 4-4, 5-5, and 6-6 are invalid,

In the next section I will show how this list narrows down to 77 combinations. Later we will how these combinations are used.

The Perimeter Method BLTR continued

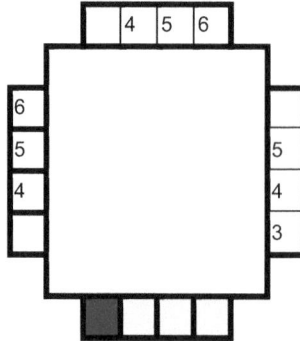

Row 1 Column 3

Place A Queen at Row 1 Column 3.

Note that the four corners and all "in 2 from the corner" positions are done in previous steps.
We will create a listing of all combinations where Row 1 Column 3 is held constant.

The complete list of possibilities will be 3 Left openings times 3 Top openings, times 3 Right openings, for a total of 27. Again we will reject combinations that have diagonal conflicts between the Left and Top, and between the Right and Top. We will also remove Left to Right row conflicts.

What remains will be 15 combinations.

The Perimeter Method
Bottom Row, Left Column
Top Row, Right Column (BLTR) continued

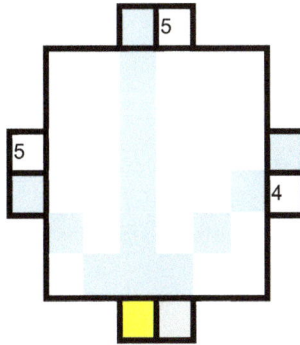

Place A Queen at Row 1 Column 4.

All the corners, column 2 and column 3 from the lower left perspective have been removed,

Only one combination remains, BLTR = 3554

When we solve for this combination, it will fail.

There are no fundamental solutions that start with a queen at Row 1 Column 4.

Potentials Row 1 Column 1

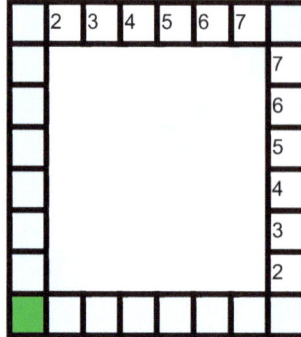

Here are the 36 combinations.

Diagonal conflicts between Top and Right are highlighted.

They can be removed from the starting list, taking us down to 30 combinations.

Here is the table of Bottom, Left, Top, and Right combinations (BLTR).

Note that Bottom and Left retain their values of Bottom 1 and Left 1.

B	L	T	R	T	R	T	R	T	R	T	R	T	R
1	1	2	2	3	2	4	2	5	2	6	2	7	2
1	1	2	3	3	3	4	3	5	3	6	3	7	3
1	1	2	4	3	4	4	4	5	4	6	4	7	4
1	1	2	5	3	5	4	5	5	5	6	5	7	5
1	1	2	6	3	6	4	6	5	6	6	6	7	6
1	1	2	7	3	7	4	7	5	7	6	7	7	7

Potentials Row 1 Column 1
Reducing the number of combinations to consider

Next consider the effects of mirroring and rotation to see if more potentials can be eliminated.
Consider these four steps.

BLTR=1132   **Now mirrored**   **Now Rotate Clock Wise**   **Conclusion BLTR 1132= BLTR 1123**

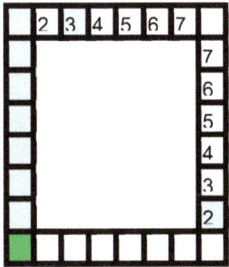

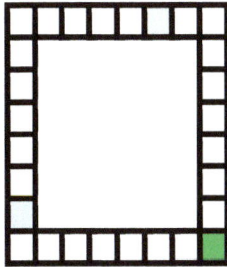

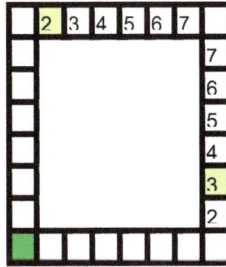

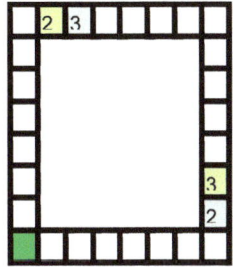

Top 2 Right 3 is a mirrored rotation of Top 3 Right 2 when bottom and left are 1.

This means we only need to test one of these two combinations.

This same logic further narrows down the potentials for the bottom row queen = 1-1

This logic will reduce our list down to 15 potentials.

B	L	T	R	T	R	T	R	T	R	T	R	T	R
1	1	2	2	3	2	4	2	5	2	6	2	7	2
1	1	2	3	3	3	4	3	5	3	6	3	7	3
1	1	2	4	3	4	4	4	5	4	6	4	7	4
1	1	2	5	3	5	4	5	5	5	6	5	7	5
1	1	2	6	3	6	4	6	5	6	6	6	7	6
1	1	2	7	3	7	4	7	5	7	6	7	7	7

Logically, at most 15 solutions need be tested to find all fundamental solutions for row 1 column 1.

Potentials: Row 1 Column 2

The next table shows how to derive potential starting points when there is a queen at row 1,
column 2, also referred to as position 102.

Left row to right row conflicts, and diagonal conflicts between the two side columns and top row are removed. In the following table, the conflicts are highlighted in blue.

My perimeter method found 8 fundamental solutions, not 7.

The additional solution is highlighted in green. It is BLTR 2442.

If you plot BLTR 2442, then rotate once clockwise, you get BLTR 2745. Either of these could be considered a fundamental, this method identifies both. The final step in the program is to un-duplicate the final file to get the correct number of total solutions.

What remains are 77 potential solutions for Row 1, Column 2.

Testing all these possible starting positions means we will find all the 7 fundamentals solutions for this position (plus one!).

Table of the 77 potential starting values when a queen is in square 102, Row 1, Col 2

Bottom Row, Left Column, Top Row, Right Column (BLTR)

B	L	T	R	L	T	R	L	T	R	L	T	R	L	T	R
2	3	3	2	4	3	2	5	3	2	6	3	2	7	3	2
2	3	3	3	4	3	3	5	3	3	6	3	3	7	3	3
2	3	3	4	4	3	4	5	3	4	6	3	4	7	3	4
2	3	3	5	4	3	5	5	3	5	6	3	5	7	3	5
2	3	3	6	4	3	6	5	3	6	6	3	6	7	3	6
2	3	4	2	4	4	2	5	4	2	6	4	2	7	4	2
2	3	4	3	4	4	3	5	4	3	6	4	3	7	4	3
2	3	4	4	4	4	4	5	4	4	6	4	4	7	4	4
2	3	4	5	4	4	5	5	4	5	6	4	5	7	4	5
2	3	4	6	4	4	6	5	4	6	6	4	6	7	4	6
2	3	5	2	4	5	2	5	5	2	6	5	2	7	5	2
2	3	5	3	4	5	3	5	5	3	6	5	3	7	5	3
2	3	5	4	4	5	4	5	5	4	6	5	4	7	5	4
2	3	5	5	4	5	5	5	5	5	6	5	5	7	5	5
2	3	5	6	4	5	6	5	5	6	6	5	6	7	5	6
2	3	6	2	4	6	2	5	6	2	6	6	2	7	6	2
2	3	6	3	4	6	3	5	6	3	6	6	3	7	6	3
2	3	6	4	4	6	4	5	6	4	6	6	4	7	6	4
2	3	6	5	4	6	5	5	6	5	6	6	5	7	6	5
2	3	6	6	4	6	6	5	6	6	6	6	6	7	6	6
2	3	7	2	4	7	2	5	7	2	6	7	2	7	7	2
2	3	7	3	4	7	3	5	7	3	6	7	3	7	7	3
2	3	7	4	4	7	4	5	7	4	6	7	4	7	7	4
2	3	7	5	4	7	5	5	7	5	6	7	5	7	7	5
2	3	7	6	4	7	6	5	7	6	6	7	6	7	7	6

Potentials Row 1 Column 3

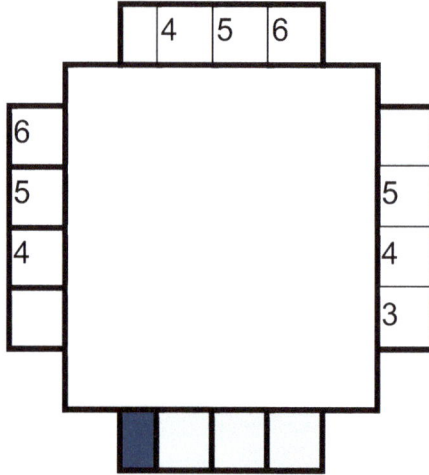

Start by listing all the combinations of bottom, left, top, and right.
Remove all row and diagonal conflicts. Highlight them in blue.
Are the fundamentals still in the remaining potentials? Highlight them in yellow.

What remains are 15 **potential** combinations to test in order to find the **3 fundamental** solutions.

Bottom	Left	Top	Right	Left	Top	Right	Left	Top	Right
3	4	4	3	5	4	3	6	4	3
3	4	4	4	5	4	4	6	4	4
3	4	4	5	5	4	5	6	4	5
3	4	5	3	5	5	3	6	5	3
3	4	5	4	5	5	4	6	5	4
3	4	5	5	5	5	5	6	5	5
3	4	6	3	5	6	3	6	6	3
3	4	6	4	5	6	4	6	6	4
3	4	6	5	5	6	5	6	6	5

Potentials: Row 1 Column 3 continued

Again, the method has added three fundamentals to the list, here highlighted in green.

This is why need to un-duplicate our final file to get the correct total number.

3443 is a rotation of 3645.

3653 is a rotation of 3664, which is a rotation of 3563.

These additional fundamentals are vexing. In an update to the perimeter method at a later date I hope to have a simple solution to avoid them. The current method is to un-duplicate the totals file with the unique setting.

Potentials: Row 1 Column 4

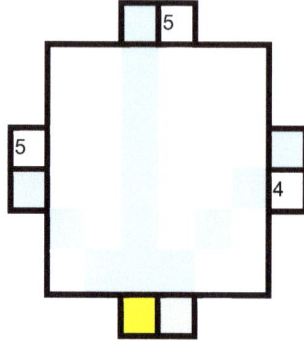

This one is dead easy!

Since we have eliminated all the corners, 2 in from the corners and 3 in from the corners, there is only one potential solution left to test.

There are no conflicts between the left and right columns, and no diagonal conflict exists between the left and top or between the top and right.

There is **1 potential** solution, but we will find during testing that it fails.

There are no **fundamental** solutions.

Bottom	Left	Top	Right
4	5	5	4

Test Your Ideas
A Winning Combination

One random example of potential starting points on an 8 x 8 grid would be **BLTR 1153**
Plot them individually, showing what is protected by each queen, then overlay them.

Plot 1-1   Plot 3-8   Plot 8-5   **BLTR = 1153**
                                                * Note Row 5 Col 7

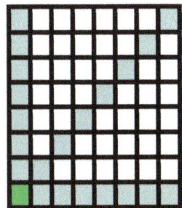 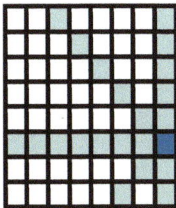 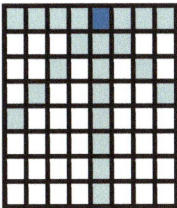 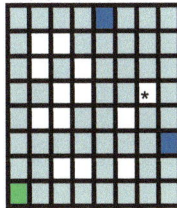

1 - - - - - -   - - - - - - 3   - - - 8 - - -   1 - - 8 - - 3

Look at the **Combined** grid. We must have one and only one queen per column, and there is only one open square in column 7, row 5. Make that a queen and see what happens.

Combined

* Note Row 2, Col 6   * Note Row 6, Col 4   * Note 4-3 and 7-2   Final solution

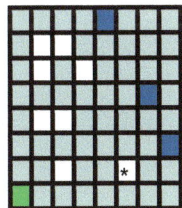 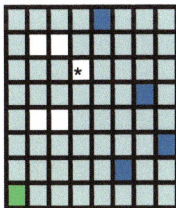 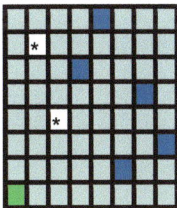 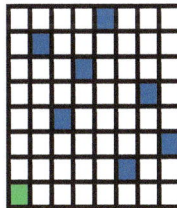

1 - - - 8 - 5 3   1 - - - 8 2 5 3   1 - - 6 8 2 5 3   1 7 4 6 8 2 5 3

RECAP:

We protected bottom row, right column, top row, and left column at **BLTR 1153**

We found that a queen had to occupy Column 7, Row 5.

We plotted this new queen and the new queen's protected squares.

We repeated this logic to complete a correct solution. We treat this as a fundamental solution.

We write that solution into the file of good solutions, along with each of this fundamental solution's rotations and each mirrored rotations.

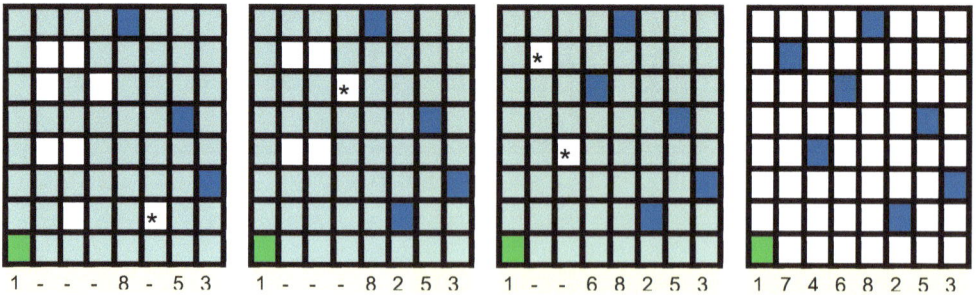

1 - - - 8 - 5 3   1 - - - 8 2 5 3   1 - - 6 8 2 5 3   1 7 4 6 8 2 5 3

Test Your Ideas
A Failing Combination

Another random example of potential starting points on an 8 x 8 grid would be
BLTR=2772

Plot them individually, showing what is protected by each queen, then overlay them.

Plot Bottom 2   Plot Left 7   Plot Top 7   Plot Right 2

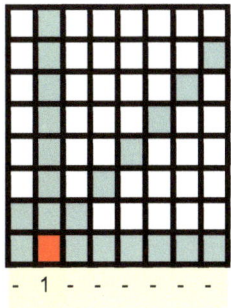 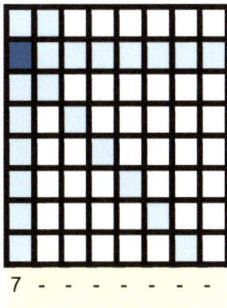 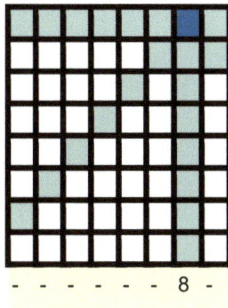 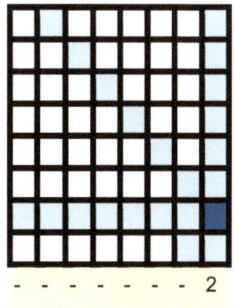

- 1 - - - - -   7 - - - - - -   - - - - - 8 -   - - - - - - 2

It starts off valid, the queens do not conflict with each other. There are four open
squares for queens. However, Rows 4 and 5 and blocked, and columns 4 and 5 are
blocked. Also, if you place a queen in any one of the open squares, the rules of
protections (row, column, and diagonal) will eliminate the remaining three openings,
leaving more dead columns or dead rows. This is a failed solution.

Combined

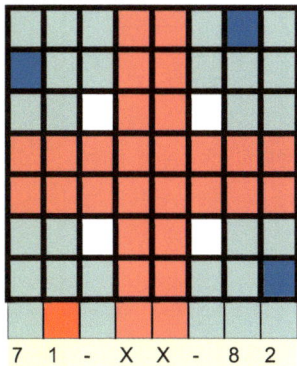

Note that this combination has dead columns and
dead rows.

A single queen must be present on each row and
column,

This is a failed solution.

7 1 - X X - 8 2

Writing the Code

I will write code for this Perimeter Method design in the C++ language.

Code::Blocks has a great open source IDE, and comes with GCC, an open source C++ compiler.

I am developing this on an HP Stream with a USB hard drive. Win 10 operating system.

I will include the code in the appendix, but here I will walk through some functions, classes, etc.

If you wish to avoid a lot of typing and debugging, you can email me at hult.norm@gmail.com and request a copy of the source code.

Here is a list of the #include files that are being used in the program:

```cpp
#include <iostream>
#include <fstream>
#include <string>
#include <vector>
#include <sstream>
#include <iostream>
#include <ios>
#include <algorithm>
#include <bits/stdc++.h>
#include <math.h>

using namespace std;

const int nsquares = 8 ;
const int rowscale = 100 ;
```

The integer variable "nsquares" is set here to 8. It can be changed from 4 to 15 to test the results.

The integer variable "rowscale" is set to 100, it is used to multiple the row number in calculating position.

class square

The class called "square" has all the values related to a single square.

The function setValues is used to calculate all the variables related to a single square on
the board.

The function printValues sends values of square to the console, which is useful for debugging.

```cpp
class square {
    public:
    int pos, row, col, rdiag, ldiag;

    void setValues( int p ) {
        pos = p;
        row = p / rowscale ;
        col = p % rowscale ;
        rdiag = row+(nsquares-col) + 1;
        ldiag = col+row;
    }
    void printValues( void) {
        cout << "pos " << pos << endl;
        cout << "row " << row << endl;
        cout << "col " << col << endl;
        cout << "ldiag " << ldiag << endl;
        cout << "rdiag " << rdiag << endl;
    }
};
```

class board

The board class is used to track which rows are protected, which columns are protected, and which left and right diagonals are protected. It also has functionality to count the number of remaining open squares by row and column.

It contains a function called "newboard" which sets up arrays and initializes them.

```
class board {
  public:
    int rrow[nsquares+1];
    int rcol[nsquares+1];
    int rrdiag[nsquares*2];
    int rldiag[nsquares*2];
    int ropenrow[nsquares+1];
    int ropencol[nsquares+1];

    void newboard( int nrows ) {
      // create arrays for available rows and columns
      for( int i=0; i<=nrows; i++ ) {
          rrow[i]=1;
          rcol[i]=1;
          ropenrow[i]=0;
          ropencol[i]=0;
      }
      for( int i=0;i<nrows*2;i++)
      {
          rrdiag[i]=1;
          rldiag[i]=1;
      }
    }
```

class board continued

Next, the board class contains a function to be used when you try to place a queen on the board.

It checks to see that the row, column, and both diagonals are free. If so, it updates the arrays to show a queen protecting that area. If the position is not free, it returns a code to indicate that the queen placement was not a success.

```
int placeQueen( square tsq ) {
    if( rrow[tsq.row]==1 &&
        rcol[tsq.col]==1 &&
        rrdiag[tsq.rdiag]==1 &&
        rldiag[tsq.ldiag]==1 )
    {
        rrow[tsq.row]=0;
        rcol[tsq.col]=0;
        rrdiag[tsq.rdiag]=0;
        rldiag[tsq.ldiag]=0;
        return 0;
    }else{
        return -1;
    }
}
```

Class board continued

Next is a long and complicated function called "countOpen". It serves several functions.

First it loops through the rows and columns, skipping protected ones and counting how many unprotected (open) squares there are by row and column.

If it detects a dead row or column, meaning there is no queen and there are no open squares to place a queen, it returns the code -1. This means that the potential solution won't work, it can be written to rejects and we can move on.

```
int countOpen( void ) {
        // returns -1 for dead row or col, 0 if no solution found, or position of next queen
        for(int i=0;i<=nsquares;i++) { ropenrow[i]=0; ropencol[i]=0; }

        // Walk the board, loop once per row, once per col;
        for(int ir=1;ir<=nsquares;ir++) {
          if( rrow[ir] == 0 ) { ropenrow[ir]=nsquares+1; }

          for( int ic=1;ic<=nsquares;ic++) {
            if( rcol[ic] == 0 ) { ropencol[ic]=nsquares+1; }

            int rdiag = ir+(nsquares-ic)+1;
            int ldiag = ic+ir;

            if( rrdiag[rdiag] == 0 || rldiag[ldiag] == 0 ||
              rrow[ir] == 0 || rcol[ic] == 0 ) {
                ropenrow[ir]++;
                ropencol[ic]++;
            }

          }
        }
        // check for dead row or dead col
        for( int i=1; i<=nsquares; i++ ) {
          if( ropenrow[i]==nsquares ) { return -1 ; }
          if( ropencol[i]==nsquares ) { return -1 ; }
        }
```

class board continued

The countOpen function will next check if there is a single open column by row, and if so that single open square must be a queen. If it is, it attempts to place the queen on the board and returns to the calling code the positional value of the new queen.

Lastly, the countOpen function checks if there is a single open column by column, and if so that single open square must be a queen. If it is, it attempts to place the queen on the board and returns to the calling code the positional value of the new queen.

```cpp
// pick a single open row or col and add to potential queens
for( int ir=1;ir<=nsquares+1;ir++) {
    if( ropenrow[ir] == nsquares-1 ) {
        // there has to be a queen i this row
        for( int ic=1;ic<nsquares+1;ic++) {
            if( rcol[ic]==0) { continue; }
            square tsq;
            int pos=(ir*rowscale) + ic;
            tsq.setValues( pos );
            int ret=placeQueen(tsq);
            if( ret<0 ) {continue;}
            // queen placed on board, add position to string;
            return pos;
        }
    }
}
for( int ic=1;ic<=nsquares+1;ic++) {
    if( ropencol[ic] == nsquares-1 ) {
        // there has to be a queen in this col;
        for( int ir=1;ir<nsquares+1;ir++) {
            if( rrow[ir]==0) { continue; }
            square tsq;
            int pos=(ir*rowscale) + ic;
            tsq.setValues( pos );
            int ret=placeQueen(tsq);
            if( ret<0 ) {continue;}
            // queen placed on board, add position to string;
            return pos;
        }
    }
}
return 0;

}
```

class board continued

Lastly, the class board contains a function used in debugging the code, called printValues.

That is the end of the class called board.

The classes square and board are the only two classes used in the code.

```
void printValues(void) {
        cout << endl << "board " << endl << endl;
        cout << "rows : " << endl;
        for(int i=1;i<=nsquares;i++) { cout << rrow[i] << " "; }
        cout << endl << "cols : "<< endl;
        for(int i=1;i<=nsquares;i++) { cout << rcol[i] << " "; }
        cout << endl << "rdiag : "<< endl;
        for(int i=1;i<=nsquares*2;i++) { cout << rrdiag[i] << " "; }
        cout << endl << "ldiag : "<< endl;
        for(int i=1;i<=nsquares*2;i++) { cout << rldiag[i] << " "; }
    }
```

The main function

Every C++ program has a function called "main". It is the controlling function of the program. It is where execution of the code begins and ends. The main function calls all the programs other functions.

```cpp
int main(void)
{
   cout << "combos " << endl;
   combos( ) ;

   cout << "solve " << endl;
   int solveRet = solve();

   cout << "totals " << endl;
   totals();

   cout << "final " << endl;
   finalfile();

   cout << endl << "complete, press any key " << endl;
   cin.ignore();

   return solveRet;

}
```

The combos function

The combos function creates the list of 108 starting values and places them in a file called "a.combos.txt".

Later, the program will open this file in append mode and add 96 more lines to this file.

If for example, the program reads in three starting positions, goes through the solve steps and finds that the solution doesn't fail for dead rows or columns, but it also doesn't fully solve, it will find the row with the fewest openings.

If there are two opening squares, the code will add two lines to the combos file.

These new lines contain the starting three queens and one new potential for each.

In the end, your combos.txt file, run on an 8x8 grid starts with 108 lines and ends with 204 lines.

```cpp
int combos( void )
{
    ofstream fcomb( "a_combos.txt") ;
    if( ! fcomb ) {
        cout << "file a_combos.txt error" ;
        return -1;
    }

    // the corner
     for( int bCol=1;bCol<2;bCol++){
        int bPos =   rowscale + bCol ;
        for( int lRow=1;lRow<2;lRow++){
            for( int rRow=bCol+1;rRow<(nsquares+1 -bCol);rRow++ ){
                int rPos = ( rowscale * rRow ) + nsquares ;
                for( int tCol=rRow+1; tCol<nsquares+1 - bCol;tCol++){
                    int tPos = ( rowscale * nsquares ) + tCol ;
                    fcomb << bPos << " " << rPos << " " << tPos <<  endl;
                }
            }
        }
     }

    int midpoint=0;
    if( nsquares % 2  == 0 ){ midpoint = nsquares / 2 ; }
    else                    { midpoint = (nsquares / 2 ) + 1 ; }

     for( int bCol = 2 ; bCol <= midpoint ; bCol++ ) {
        int bPos =   rowscale + bCol ;
        for( int lRow = bCol + 1 ; lRow <= nsquares+1 - bCol ; lRow++ ) {
            int lPos = ( rowscale * lRow ) + 1 ;
            for( int rRow = bCol ; rRow < nsquares+1 - bCol ; rRow++ )  {
                int rPos = ( rowscale * rRow ) + nsquares ;
                for( int tCol=bCol+1; tCol<=nsquares+1 - bCol;tCol++ ) {
                    int tPos = ( rowscale * nsquares ) + tCol ;
                    // some exclusions based on same row, or same diagonal
                    if( lRow == rRow )                      { continue; }
                    if( tCol == rRow )                      { continue; }
                    if( tCol == nsquares + 1 - lRow )    { continue; }
                    cout   << bCol << " " << rRow << " "
                           << tCol << " " << lRow << endl;
                    fcomb << bPos << " " << rPos << " "
                          << tPos << " " << lPos << endl;
                }
            }
        }
    }
    return 0;
}
```

The solve function

The solve function begins by opening the necessary files, and it ends by closing those files.

Note that the a_combos.txt file is opened with two handles. The handle "istarts" is the input file of staring values, "i" is for input. The handle "astarts" is also the a_combos.txt file, this time opened in append mode. The "a" is for append.

This function creates the file "c_fundamentals.txt". As pointed out earlier, some additional rotations may creep into this file, so in the end it will contain more than the pure number of fundamentals. In an 8x8 grid there are 12 true fundamentals, but this file will contain 16 lines.

This file also creates the file "d_fails.txt". This file will contain the words "dead row or column" and the list of starting values that came from the a_combos.txt file, but they were rejected in the solve process.

The last file created here is "f_totals.txt". It will contain all of the found solutions, including all rotations, mirrors, and mirrored rotations. There will be duplicates, so as a last step we sort the f_totals.txt file out to g_final.txt, which will contain our 92 total solutions.

The main purpose of this function is to read a_combos.txt one line at a time.

It then passes this line, along with the append file handle, to the function resolve.

The return value of this call will be used to determine where the line ends up.

A return value of 0 is a successful solution, all queens placed on the board. The line is written to the file c_fundamentals.txt.

A return value of -1 means that this solution is bad – there is a dead row or a dead column, meaning all the squares in that row or column are protected, but there is no queen. These go to the d_fails.txt file.

A return value of -9 means an attempt was made to place the queen in a protected square. These also go to the d_fails.txt file.

A return value of 1 means that two or more rows have been appended to the a_combos.txt file. The function then goes to the next line from a_combos.txt, and will eventually read these new lines and run them through the process.

```cpp
int solve( void )
{
    ifstream istarts(  "a_combos.txt"    ) ;
    ofstream astarts( "a_combos.txt" , ios::app ) ;
    ofstream funds( "c_fundamentals.txt" ) ;
    ofstream tots ( "f_totals.txt"       ) ;
    ofstream fails( "d_fails.txt"         ) ;

    if( ! istarts || ! astarts || ! funds || ! tots  || ! fails  ) {
        cout << "a file has failed to open " << endl ;
        return -1;
    }

    string instring;
    string bPos = "0" ;
    string prev_bPos;

    while(  getline(istarts,instring)  ) {
        if( istarts.eof() ) { break;}
        if( istarts.peek()!='\n') {
            int resret = resolve( instring, astarts );

            if( resret == 0 ) {
             bPos = instring.substr( 0, instring.find(" ") );
             if( bPos > prev_bPos ) { prev_bPos = bPos; }
                cout << "success! " << instring << '\r' ;
                funds << instring << endl;
            }
            else if( resret == -1 ) {
             fails << "dead row or col " << instring << endl;
            }
            else if( resret == -9 ) {
             fails << "couldn't place queen on board " << instring << endl;
            }
            else if( resret ==1 ) { // new lines added to a_combos.txt, keep
looping }
            instring.clear();
            istarts.clear();
             }
        }
    }
    istarts.close();
    astarts.close();
    funds.close();
    tots.close();
    fails.close();
    return 0;
}
```

The resolve function

The resolve function does a lot of the heavy lifting in this program.

The line read in from a_combos.txt, as well as the append file handle for the a_combos.txt file are passed into the resolve function.

It first reads the positions into an array.

If that array is complete, in other words if it contains 8 queens for an 8x8 grid, it returns to the solve function with a value of 0.

It then creates an object from the board class, named brd. It uses the newboard function to set up the board.

Then for each position, the resolve function declares a square from the class square, and uses the setValues function to determine row, column, left and right diagonals.

Next it attempts to place the queen on the board. If any of these attempts fail, resolve returns to the solve function with a code -9.

It then calls the brd objects countOpen function. If countOpen returns a -1 code, this means that there is a dead row or dead column, and this -1 code is passed back to the calling solve function.

If we get this far, meaning we have not succeeded and returned the 0, we have not failed to place a queen and returned -9, and we have not encountered a dead row or column and returned a -1, we go on to the next step,

If countOpen returned a value of 0, this means that no new queens were determined, and no problems were encountered. In this situation, we find the row with the lowest number of open squares, and for each open square we add append a line to the end of the a_combos.txt file with the starting line and the new position appended to the end. There will always be a minimum of two new lines added. We then return the value of 1 to the solve function.

If the countOpen function returned a value greater than 0, this is a really good thing, we have found a new queen! This means a row or column only had one open square left, and since every row or square has to have a queen, this open square must be one. This doesn't mean the solution is going to work out, we have to add this queen to the line that was passed to the function, then use the C++ goto to go back to the top of this function and work it through.

```
int resolve( string& instring, ofstream& astarts ) {
TOP:
    stringstream stream(instring);
    int qray[nsquares];
    for(int i=0;i<nsquares;i++) {qray[i]=0;}
    int index=0;
    int n;
    while(stream>>n) {
        qray[index]=n;
        index++;
        if(index==nsquares) {break;}
    }
    if( index==nsquares ) { /* success! */ return 0; }
    square tsq;
    board brd;
    brd.newboard(nsquares);
    for(int i=0;i<nsquares;i++) {
        if( qray[i]==0 ) { continue; }
        tsq.setValues(qray[i]);
        int pret = brd.placeQueen( tsq ) ;
        if( pret == 0 ) { /* all is well */ } else { return -9; }
    }
    // the potential queens are on the board, check open counts;
    int chkret = brd.countOpen( );
    if( chkret == -1 ) { /* dead row or column */ return -1; }
    else if( chkret==0 ) {
        // no dead rows or cols, no single queen square found
        // find row with fewest open squares, for each one add to the
potqueens file
        int min=rowscale;
        int minindex=0;
        for( int i=1; i<=nsquares; i++ ) {
            if( brd.ropenrow[i] < min ) { min=brd.ropenrow[i]; minindex=i; }
        }
        for( int ic=1;ic<nsquares+1;ic++) {
            if( brd.rcol[ic] == 0 ) { continue; }
            int pos=(minindex*rowscale) + ic;
            astarts << instring << " " << pos << endl;
        }
        return 1;
    }
    else if( chkret > 0 ) {
        // new queen placed on the board, add it to the string, got to top of
resolve function
        instring += " ";
        instring += patch::to_string(chkret) ;
        goto TOP;
    }
    return 0;
}
```

The totals function

The totals function is used to read in the c_fundamentals.txt file and create the f_totals file.

For each line read in from c_fundamentals text, this function performs these steps.

> Read in a line from c_fundamentals.txt.
>
> Place the queens read in into an array.
>
> Sort the array. Since rows are scaled by a factor of 100, this puts them in row order.
>
> Write that line to the f_totals.txt file.
>
> Loop three times:
>
> > Call the rotatecw function (rotate clockwise)
> > Sort the returned array.
> > Write it to the f_totals.txt file.
>
> After 3 times, call the rotatecw one more time to return to the starting position.
>
> Call the mirrorbrd (mirror the board) function, write that to the f_totals file.
>
> Loop three times (we need to get the mirroed rotations).
>
> > Call the rotatecw function (rotate clockwise)
> > Sort the returned array.
> > Write it to the f_totals.txt file.

Close all the files, and we are done!

Note that f_totals.txt will contain some duplicates.

```cpp
int totals( void ) {
    ofstream tots ( "f_totals.txt"        ) ;
    ifstream funds( "c_fundamentals.txt" ) ;
    if( ! funds || ! tots  ) { return -1 ;}
    string instring;
    int qray[nsquares] ;
    while( getline(funds,instring)  ) {
        if( funds.eof()  ) {break;}
        if( funds.peek()!='\n') {
            stringstream stream(instring);
            for(int i=0;i<nsquares;i++) { qray[i] = 0 ; }
            int index=0;
            int n;
            while(stream>>n) {
                qray[index]=n;
                index++;
                if(index==nsquares) {break;}
            }
            int sizen = sizeof(qray) / sizeof(qray[0]) ;
            sort( qray, qray + sizen );
            int cwray[nsquares];
            // write out fundamental
            for( int x=0;x<nsquares;x++ ) { tots << qray[x] << " " ; }
            tots << endl;
                for( int z=0; z<3; z++ ) { // write out 3 rotations
                rotatecw( qray, cwray );
                sort( cwray, cwray + sizen );
                for( int x=0;x<nsquares;x++ ) {
                        qray[x]=cwray[x]; tots << qray[x] << " ";
                }
                tots << endl;
            }
            // rotate back to fundamental
            rotatecw( qray, cwray );
            sort( cwray, cwray + sizen );
            for( int z=0;z<nsquares;z++ ) { qray[z]=cwray[z]; }
            mirrorbrd( qray, cwray ) ;
             for( int x=0;x<nsquares;x++ ) { tots << cwray[x] << " "; }
             tots << endl;
            for( int z=0;z<nsquares;z++ ) { qray[z]=cwray[z]; }
            for( int z=0; z<3; z++ ) { // write out 3 rotations
                rotatecw( qray, cwray );
                sort( cwray, cwray + sizen );
                for( int x=0;x<nsquares;x++ ) {
                        qray[x]=cwray[x]; tots << qray[x] << " " ;
                }
                tots << endl;
            }
        }
    }
    tots.close();
    funds.close();
    return 0;
}
```

```
int getpos( int r, int c)
{
    int pos = (r * rowscale) + c;
    return pos;
}
int getrdiag( int row, int col )
{
    return row+(nsquares-col) + 1;
}
int getldiag( int row, int col )
{
    return col+row;
}
int clockwise( int pos ) {
    int row = pos / rowscale ;
    int col = pos % rowscale ;
    int newrow = (nsquares+1)-col;
    int newcol = row ;
    int newpos = ( newrow * rowscale ) + newcol;
    return newpos;
}
int mirror( int pos ) {
    // side to side mirror
    int row = pos / rowscale ;
    int col = pos % rowscale ;
    int newcol = (nsquares+1)-col ;
    int newpos = ( row * rowscale ) + newcol;
    return newpos;
}
void rotatecw( int* qray, int* outray )
{
  for( int i=0;i<nsquares;i++ )  {
    if(qray[i]>0) { outray[i]=clockwise(qray[i]) ; }
  }
}
void mirrorbrd( int* qray, int* outray )
{
  for( int i=0;i<nsquares;i++ )  {
    outray[i]=mirror(qray[i]) ;
  }
}
int finalfile()
{
    system("sort /unique f_totals.txt /output g_final.txt" );
    return 0;
}
```

These functions are self-explanatory.

They perform tasks such as determining a square's position, and determining the right or left diagonal.

The clockwise function moves a single square once clockwise.

The mirror function mirrors a single square left or right on a row.

The rotatecw function rotates an entire board via an array once clockwise.

The mirrorbrd function mirrors the entire board.

The finalfile function calls on a Windows command to sort the file unique.

Appendix – The Solutions

Fundamental 1

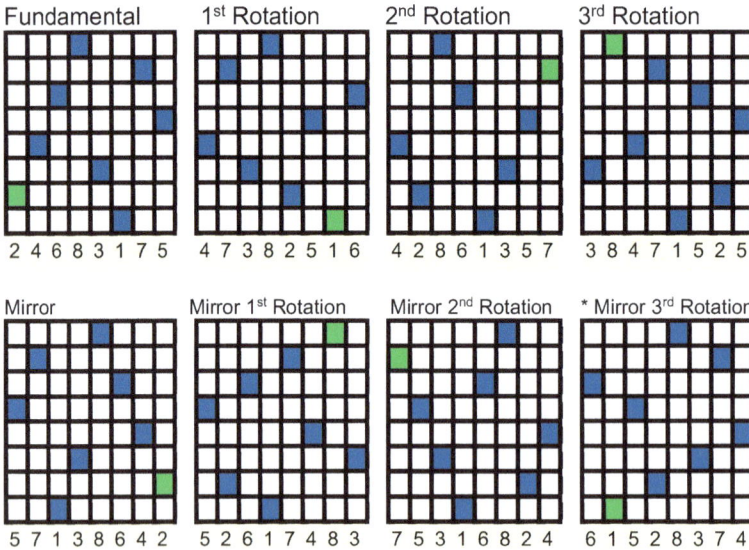

Fundamental	1st Rotation	2nd Rotation	3rd Rotation
2 4 6 8 3 1 7 5	4 7 3 8 2 5 1 6	4 2 8 6 1 3 5 7	3 8 4 7 1 5 2 5

Mirror	Mirror 1st Rotation	Mirror 2nd Rotation	* Mirror 3rd Rotation
5 7 1 3 8 6 4 2	5 2 6 1 7 4 8 3	7 5 3 1 6 8 2 4	6 1 5 2 8 3 7 4

* Note that if you consider the Mirrored 3rd Rotation instead as the fundamental, it fits our theory that all fundamentals can be found by looking at Row 1, columns 1,2,3,4.

Fundamental 2

Fundamental

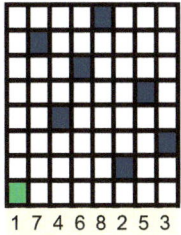

1 7 4 6 8 2 5 3

1ˢᵗ Rotation

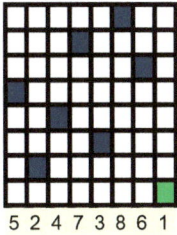

5 2 4 7 3 8 6 1

2ⁿᵈ Rotation

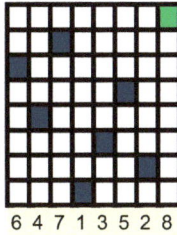

6 4 7 1 3 5 2 8

3ʳᵈ Rotation

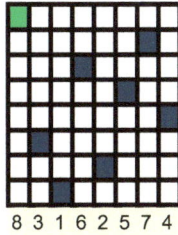

8 3 1 6 2 5 7 4

Mirror

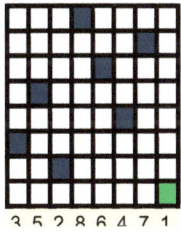

3 5 2 8 6 4 7 1

Mirror 1ˢᵗ Rotation

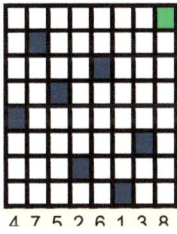

4 7 5 2 6 1 3 8

Mirror 2ⁿᵈ Rotation

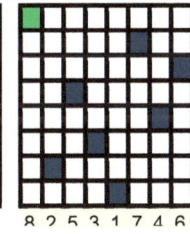

8 2 5 3 1 7 4 6

Mirror 3ʳᵈ Rotation

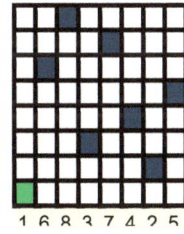

1 6 8 3 7 4 2 5

Fundamental 3

Fundamental

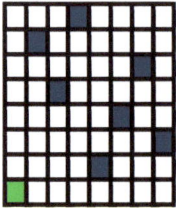

1 7 5 8 2 4 6 3

1st Rotation

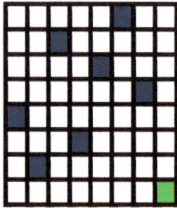

4 2 7 3 6 8 5 1

2nd Rotation

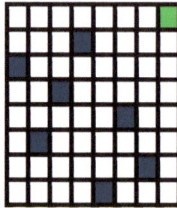

6 3 5 7 1 4 2 8

3rd Rotation

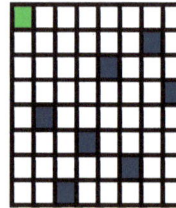

8 4 1 3 6 2 7 5

Mirror

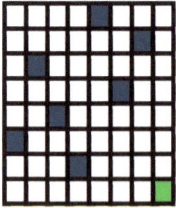

3 6 4 2 8 5 7 1

Mirror 1st Rotation

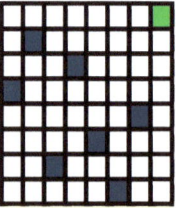

5 7 2 6 3 1 4 8

Mirror 2nd Rotation

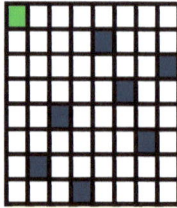

8 2 4 1 7 5 3 6

Mirror 3rd Rotation

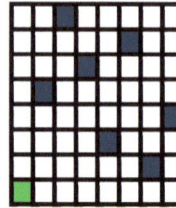

1 5 8 6 3 7 2 4

Fundamental 4

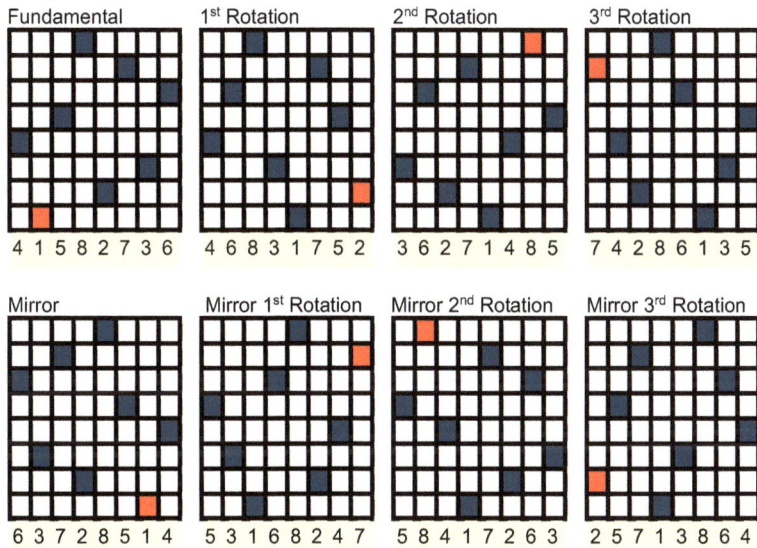

Fundamental	1st Rotation	2nd Rotation	3rd Rotation
4 1 5 8 2 7 3 6	4 6 8 3 1 7 5 2	3 6 2 7 1 4 8 5	7 4 2 8 6 1 3 5

Mirror	Mirror 1st Rotation	Mirror 2nd Rotation	Mirror 3rd Rotation
6 3 7 2 8 5 1 4	5 3 1 6 8 2 4 7	5 8 4 1 7 2 6 3	2 5 7 1 3 8 6 4

Fundamental 5

Fundamental	1st Rotation	2nd Rotation	3rd Rotation
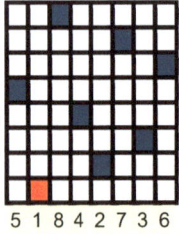	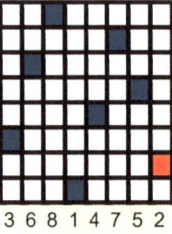	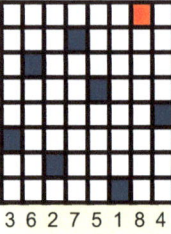	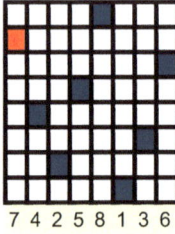
5 1 8 4 2 7 3 6	3 6 8 1 4 7 5 2	3 6 2 7 5 1 8 4	7 4 2 5 8 1 3 6

Mirror	Mirror 1st Rotation	Mirror 2nd Rotation	Mirror 3rd Rotation
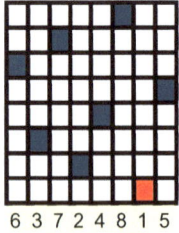	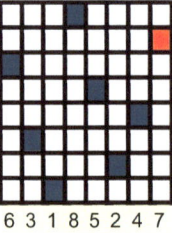	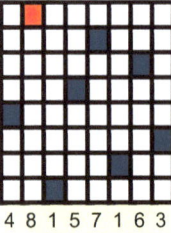	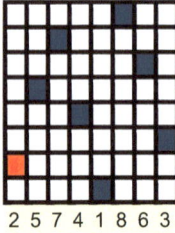
6 3 7 2 4 8 1 5	6 3 1 8 5 2 4 7	4 8 1 5 7 1 6 3	2 5 7 4 1 8 6 3

Fundamental 6

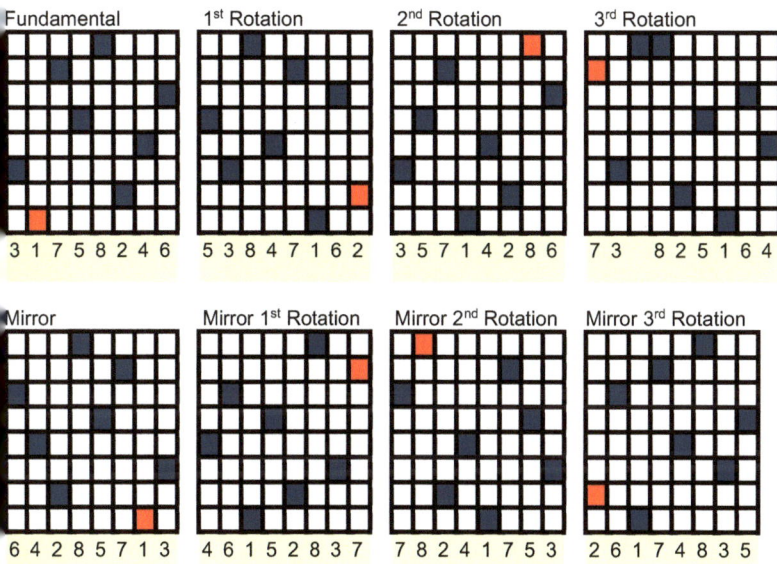

Fundamental

3 1 7 5 8 2 4 6

1st Rotation

5 3 8 4 7 1 6 2

2nd Rotation

3 5 7 1 4 2 8 6

3rd Rotation

7 3   8 2 5 1 6 4

Mirror

6 4 2 8 5 7 1 3

Mirror 1st Rotation

4 6 1 5 2 8 3 7

Mirror 2nd Rotation

7 8 2 4 1 7 5 3

Mirror 3rd Rotation

2 6 1 7 4 8 3 5

Fundamental 7

Fundamental

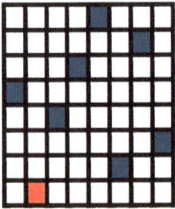

5 1 4 6 8 2 7 3

1st Rotation

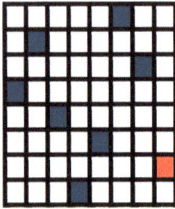

5 7 4 1 3 8 6 2

2nd Rotation

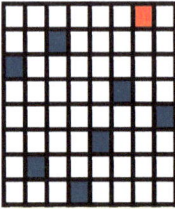

6 2 7 1 3 5 8 4

3rd Rotation

7 3　1 6 8 5 2 4

Mirror

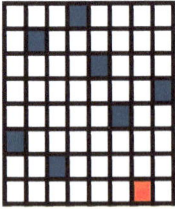

3 7 2 8 6 4 1 5

Mirror 1st Rotation

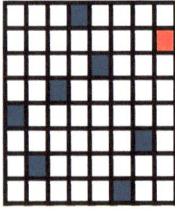

4 2 5 8 6 1 3 7

Mirror 2nd Rotation

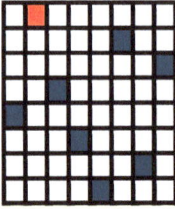

4 8 5 3 1 7 2 6

Mirror 3rd Rotation

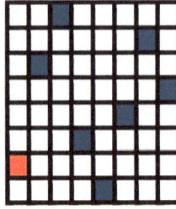

2 6 8 3 1 4 7 5

Fundamental 8

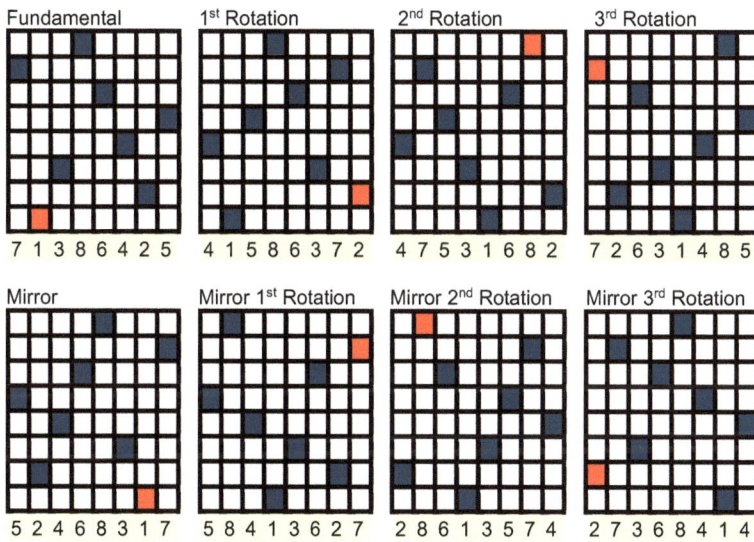

Fundamental	1st Rotation	2nd Rotation	3rd Rotation
7 1 3 8 6 4 2 5	4 1 5 8 6 3 7 2	4 7 5 3 1 6 8 2	7 2 6 3 1 4 8 5

Mirror	Mirror 1st Rotation	Mirror 2nd Rotation	Mirror 3rd Rotation
5 2 4 6 8 3 1 7	5 8 4 1 3 6 2 7	2 8 6 1 3 5 7 4	2 7 3 6 8 4 1 4

Fundamental 9

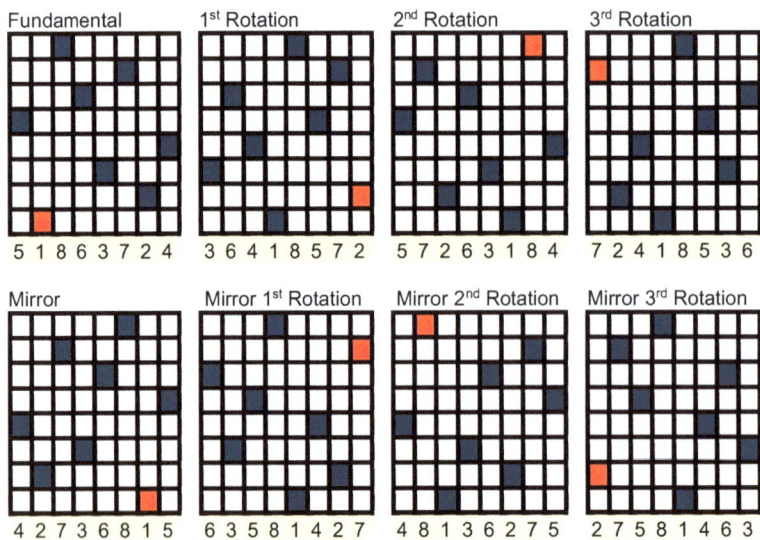

Fundamental	1st Rotation	2nd Rotation	3rd Rotation
5 1 8 6 3 7 2 4	3 6 4 1 8 5 7 2	5 7 2 6 3 1 8 4	7 2 4 1 8 5 3 6

Mirror	Mirror 1st Rotation	Mirror 2nd Rotation	Mirror 3rd Rotation
4 2 7 3 6 8 1 5	6 3 5 8 1 4 2 7	4 8 1 3 6 2 7 5	2 7 5 8 1 4 6 3

Fundamental 10

Fundamental
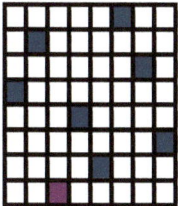
5 7 1 4 2 8 6 3

1st Rotation
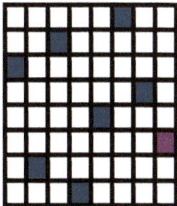
6 2 7 1 4 8 5 3

2nd Rotation
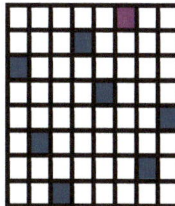
6 3 1 7 5 8 2 4

3rd Rotation
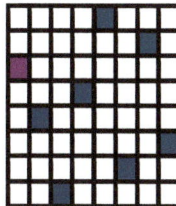
6 4 1 5 8 2 7 3

Mirror
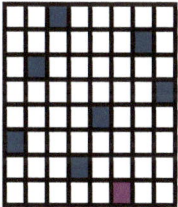
3 5 8 2 4 1 7 5

Mirror 1st Rotation
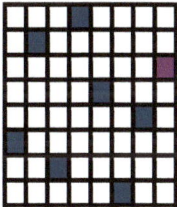
3 7 2 8 5 1 4 6

Mirror 2nd Rotation
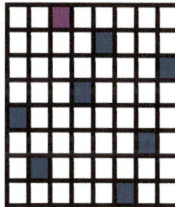
4 2 8 5 7 1 3 6

Mirror 3rd Rotation
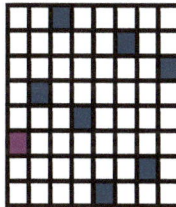
3 5 8 4 1 7 2 6

Fundamental 11

Fundamental

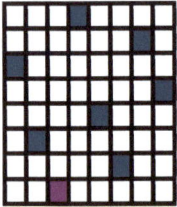

6 3 1 8 4 2 7 5

1st Rotation

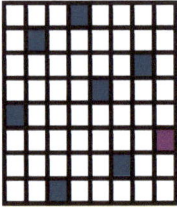

4 7 1 8 5 2 6 3

2nd Rotation

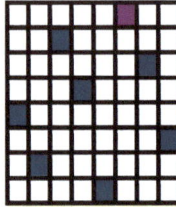

4 2 7 5 1 8 6 3

3rd Rotation

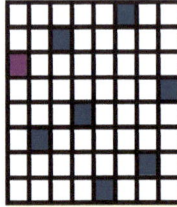

6 3 7 4 1 8 2 5

Mirror

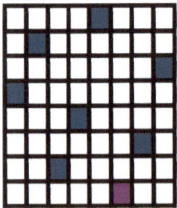

5 7 2 4 8 1 3 6

Mirror 1st Rotation

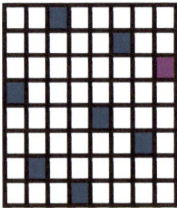

5 2 8 1 4 7 3 6

Mirror 2nd Rotation

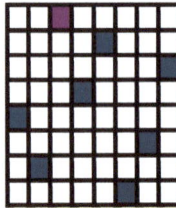

4 2 8 5 7 1 3 6

Mirror 3rd Rotation

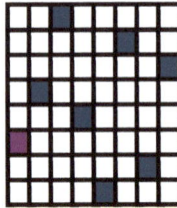

3 5 8 4 1 7 2 6

Fundamental 12

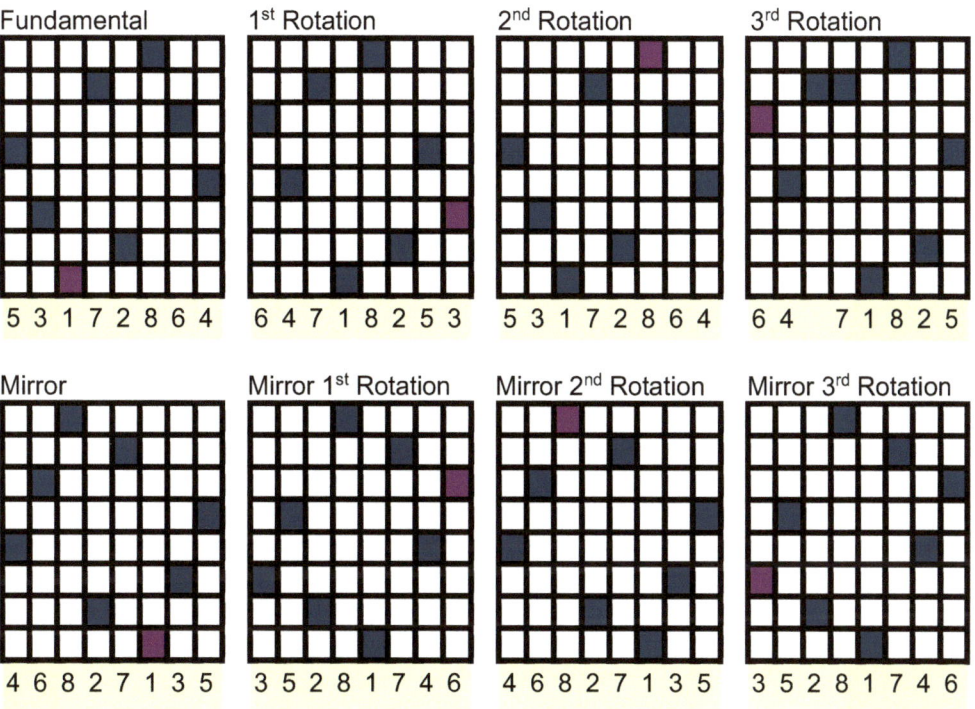

Fundamental	1st Rotation	2nd Rotation	3rd Rotation

5 3 1 7 2 8 6 4   6 4 7 1 8 2 5 3   5 3 1 7 2 8 6 4   6 4   7 1 8 2 5

Mirror	Mirror 1st Rotation	Mirror 2nd Rotation	Mirror 3rd Rotation

4 6 8 2 7 1 3 5   3 5 2 8 1 7 4 6   4 6 8 2 7 1 3 5   3 5 2 8 1 7 4 6

Note that Solution 12 is symmetrical, and so it only has 4 unique solutions, not 8.

The purple colored square is only for reference to the starting position, so think of all the squares being the same color.

The Fundamental is the same as the 2nd Rotation.
The 1st Rotation is the same as the 3rd Rotation.
The Mirror is the same as the Mirror 2nd Rotation.
The Mirror 1st Rotation is the same as the Mirror 3rd Rotation.

So there are 12 fundamentals. If each of them provided 8 solutions the total number would be 96. Because Solution 12 only has 4 unique solutions, the total number is reduced to 92.

Appendix B
Tables 4x4 to 16X16

Rows	Fundamental Solutions	Total Solutions
4	1	2
5	2	10
6	1	4
7	6	40
8	12	92
9	46	352
10	92	724
11	341	2680
12	1787	14200
13	9233	73712
14	45752	365596
15	285053	2279184
16	1846955	14772512